WAITING WITH A
Purpose

A Guide to Finding Your Boaz

Anastasia Means-Dallas

authorHOUSE®

AuthorHouse™
1663 Liberty Drive
Bloomington, IN 47403
www.authorhouse.com
Phone: 1-800-839-8640

Published by AuthorHouse 3/2/2012

ISBN: 978-1-4520-8112-0 (e)
ISBN: 978-1-4520-8111-3 (sc)

Library of Congress Control Number: 2010913863

This book is printed on acid-free paper.

All Scripture reference is from the KJV of the Bible unless otherwise noted.

Introduction

Divorce is running rampant in society today, and unfortunately the rate of divorce is steadily increasing in the Christian community. Experiencing a painful divorce and numerous failed relationships prompted me to write this book. This book will inform, warn, and provide tools and lessons that I've learned on the journey to pursuing a healthy marriage. Divorce is painful even when both parties are amicable in the situation. I ended up in a verbally abusive marriage that left me emotionally damaged, broke, and a single mother of three children struggling just to make ends meet. I fell into such a depression that some days I didn't have the desire to live. My only escape was when I would go to work as a teacher and interact with my students—then, I would forget the living hell that I was experiencing at home. I thought that I would never recover from this ordeal because when I finally left the marriage, I walked away with my children, the clothes on my back, a couple of personal items, and my faith in God. I had planned a way of escape in my head for weeks, but I was finally ready to execute.

The day I left, I was handling things without thinking about them. I went to my job and resigned from my teaching position after explaining the extenuating circumstances to my principal, I withdrew my two school-aged children from their school, I informed the babysitter of my then ten-month-old, and I closed out accounts and obtained a hotel for two days. I spent two days in the hotel to rest, as I was preparing to make the journey back home to my mom's cramped one-bedroom apartment. When I finally reached my mom's house, all I could do was cry.

My mom held me and reminded me, "Baby, it's not all lost, you still have your faith in God." The first night I was there, I was so numb. I just lay in the bed, not able to interact with my mom or my kids. I did not accept phone calls at all because I did not have the energy nor the desire to explain what was going on in my life.

After experiencing many other failed relationships along the way, I have picked up a few nuggets of wisdom. My theory is that if you can learn through someone else's mistake, there is no sense in having to go through the same thing. Life is about helping others along the way. As a matter of fact, the Bible declares, "We overcome by the blood of the lamb, and by the word of our testimony" (Revelation 12:11).

This book provides examples through the lives of three women who attract "Roaz." Roaz is simply a counterfeit "Boaz." Boaz is the ideal man, while Roaz is the type of man that you will attract when you have low self-esteem, are anxious to be married, don't have an understanding of agape love, or you simply have impure motives for wanting to be married. The different forms of Roaz described in the book you have encountered, are dating, or maybe even have married. If you find some of these characteristics in your husband, please do not pack his bags and tell him to hit the road, Jack! There is always hope if you are willing to work at improving your marriage relationship. "And we know that all things work together for good to them that love God, to them who are the called according to his purpose" (Romans 8:28).

The book starts off by giving some key principles by looking at the Biblical character Ruth to show how she obtained a godly man (Boaz). Even if you have not had good examples on love and relationships, God's word is so awesome that it will teach you whatever you missed along the way through examples in the Bible. It's amazing how many people do not like to read the word of God and obtain help for life's issues. They would rather watch the *Young and the Restless*, or the *Bold and the Beautiful*, but what they don't realize is that they will find more drama in the Bible and then experience the key to victory along the way. The biggest tactic that Satan has used on the earth is to distract God's people so that they won't have time to get into his word. Everything we need in this life can be found in the sixty-six books of the Bible. There are some key principles written in the book of Ruth for our learning. This book is geared toward helping singles; however, the married person may find some nuggets along the way as well.

Contents

Chapter 1:
The Story of Ruth

What made Ruth so special?

Then she fell on her face, and bowed herself to the ground, and said unto him, "Why have I found grace in thine eyes" (Ruth 2:10)?

The book of Ruth, although it's a small chapter in the Bible, is a powerful story of favor, redemption, and how she met the man of her dream "Boaz." Although Ruth lost her first husband, she did not move into a desperate state at all; she did not go looking for another man. However, she did position herself to receive another husband. This is truly significant because many women have moved to a state of desperation when it comes to a mate. Some women begin putting their dreams on hold, such as buying their dream home, driving a luxury vehicle, or pursuing personal goals because they are waiting on "Mr. Right." Although we may be single, it's important that we are waiting with a purpose. This type of waiting is an active waiting. We are not twiddling our thumbs, falling into a depression, or having pity parties. We are women who are making things happen. We are successful in every aspect of our lives.

Let's look at it like this—imagine a cake that has all the right ingredients, and it's baked to perfection. The cake already has everything it needs to be tasty. Someone comes along and adds some icing to that cake. This makes the cake even tastier. Single women are that cake, and the right mate is the icing. The icing did not make or define the cake, it simply made it sweeter. We will discuss further in Chapter 2 what the present-day Ruth looks like, but let's go back and take some lessons from Ruth. When the chapter opens, it shows how Ruth remains with her grieving mother-in -law because of the loss of her two precious sons (Mahloin and Kilion). The story goes on to explain how Ruth and Orpah (her sister-in-law) are left with their mother-in-law, and how Naomi admonishes both of them to return to their mother's home. Naomi bids each of them farewell and offers her blessings.

Orpah kisses her mother-in-law goodbye and leaves without hesitation. Ruth decides not only to follow Naomi back to her homeland of Bethlehem, but she also decides that she would serve the god of Naomi. The first lesson we can learn from Ruth is that she was faithful. She remained with her mother-in-law—she could have been like Orpah and left. Had Ruth left, she never would have received her blessing, her "Boaz." Although our situation may not be exactly like Ruth's, we must remain faithful to God in every area of our lives. For instance, if God has called us to work in the children's ministry, we must be faithful in that area.

Faithfulness brings about promotion and, who knows, maybe Boaz is working in the children's ministry as well. People are always watching us when we least expect.

This brings me to my next point. When Boaz discovered Ruth, she was working. She was gleaning in the field. As Ruth is gleaning in the field, she finds herself gleaning in Boaz's field. She followed the instructions of her mother-in-law, which proves she was obedient. Lesson number two—Ruth was obedient. She could have easily ignored her mother-in-law and gleaned in someone else's field. Had she not gleaned in Boaz's field, he probably would have never known who Ruth was.

After Boaz notices Ruth in his field, he is already impressed with Sister Ruth, and he has given her favor in the field. Naomi encourages Ruth take a bath, put on some sweet-smelling perfume, adorn herself in her very best outfit, and go down to the threshing floor and lie at Boaz's feet. Ruth willingly follows the instructions of her mother-in-law. This brings lesson number three—Ruth was submissive. She listened to Naomi and followed her instructions. This was important because other women were vying for Boaz's attention as well, so it was important that she stood out. The same is true today. There are definitely more men than women in some cities, such as Atlanta; however, we must possess something that makes us stand out from other women. As a godly woman, it is the beauty within that will spill over into your outward beauty.

Another thing that Ruth did before approaching Boaz was that she waited until he was in a relaxed position before she approached him. Lesson number five—Ruth possessed wisdom. Ruth gently approached him and explained to him how he was Naomi's kinsman-redeemer. (A kinsman-redeemer was significant in keeping the family line. The next male in line would normally marry a widow). The entire book of Proverbs deals with wisdom. Wisdom is the principal thing. Wisdom is important in finding a mate, and that's why it's important to have a seasoned person to impart knowledge to you and share their experiences. We could have avoided several pitfalls if we had wisdom regarding various situations.

The story unfolds by Boaz becoming the kinsman-redeemer and taking Ruth as his wife. The story is about love and redemption because Boaz saw something in Ruth that apparently stood out to him. It wasn't only her outward beauty, because I'm pretty sure she was sweaty and tired when she gleaned in the field. It shows that a man is not looking for us to have a nice figure and sit around and look pretty all day. Boaz will most likely find you in the trenches of everyday life, not in the nightclub. Sadly, some woman have focused so much on the outward beauty that they've allowed Hollywood and the women in the videos to determine how they are supposed to act or dress to get a man. Please take notice that Ruth did not wear provocative clothes, and nor did she have to manipulate Boaz in order to become his wife.

Finally, lesson number six—Ruth found favor in Boaz's eyes. This is evident because Boaz was a wealthy man who was well-established. I'm pretty sure he had the attention of most single women in that town, but it was Ruth who ended up with the prize. For example, imagine going to church and seeing a man you know is spirit-filled, a hard worker, and notably successful. Immediately, single women begin to gain his attention in some way, shape, or form. All of sudden, you find out that he's getting married. The first thing we tend to do is ask ourselves, "What did she have that I don't have?" She may not even be beautiful physically, but she certainly had one thing working for her—*favor*.

Prayer:
Father God in the name of Jesus, I thank you for the examples that you have provided for us in the Bible. It is my desire to marry, so I ask that you search my heart and show me the areas that need adjusting. I thank you for positioning me to receive a godly husband so that our marriage will bring honor to you on the earth. I thank you that I have favor with you, and favor with man. I thank you that the blessing is active in my life, and I walk in the blessing daily. Thank you, Lord, for my Boaz. In Jesus name, Amen.

Write down anything God reveals to you. It may be revealed immediately or at another time. Make sure you are listening when he speaks.

_____

_____

_____

_____

_____

Anastasia Means-Dallas

_____

_____

_____

_____

_____

_____

_____

_____

_____

_____

_____

_____

_____

_____

_____

_____

Chapter 2:
The Present-Day Ruth:
The Proverbial Woman

What does the present-day Ruth look like?

Who can find a virtuous woman? For her price is far above rubies (Proverbs 31:10).

There are many women's lives that could have been used to provide an example of a godly woman. However, Ruth stands out because her character is simple to follow, and it will aid today's women when they are in the process of waiting to be married. Ruth is a great example because she was a woman who was waiting with a purpose. This is important for the present-day single woman. The first thing that single women can take note of is that Ruth understood her purpose. This is important for today's single women because if you understand your purpose prior to getting married, you will be more selective about who you allow to come into your life. For example, if you know that your purpose is to be a motivational speaker and the mate you choose is not willing to support your vision, then division has already set in.

Secondly, another part that we can examine and learn from Ruth's character is that she knew her worth and value. Some women still have not realized that they are the apple of God's eye. The present-day Ruth needs to understand this, or she will end up tolerating things in a relationship that God never intended. For example, some women have spent so much time on decorating their outer appearance to satisfy a man that oftentimes they feel as though they have to wear provocative clothes or have sex with a man in order to secure a relationship with him.

Thirdly, Ruth was faithful. When we are faithful over a few things, God will make us ruler over many. Ruth exhibited her faithfulness by remaining with her mother-in-law until it was her season to move on and marry Boaz. The present-day Ruth must remain faithful to God by listening to and obeying his voice. For instance, if God has called you to complete a specific task or assignment, you must remain faithful where God has planted you. God placed Terry in the children's ministry at her church. She wanted to join the choir, not because she could sing, but because she felt it would be easier. Well, after being faithful in the children's ministry for just six months, she met Mike, and they were married a year later. This is an example of how faithfulness pays off.

Lastly, Ruth's motives were pure. Ruth was not looking for a husband—she was busy working. Ruth didn't exactly come out and say that she wanted a husband, but God knew her heart. She didn't manipulate Boaz, and she didn't desire to be married because her clock was ticking or so she could get away from Naomi. Many of the present-day single women want to be married for selfish reasons. They are finding themselves wanting to get married to save money, to have children, or to have sex without feeling guilty. Ruth's motives were pure, and as a result, she ended up with the man of her dreams.

Chapter 3:
The Different Forms of Roaz

Who is Roaz?

Boaz is a man of your dreams, but Roaz is something else altogether. There are many forms of Roaz that you will encounter in this book. You may be able to identify a combination of traits that Roaz possesses, or your Roaz might fit the exact description. These descriptions are based on experience and observation, and I make no apologies if it happens to fit someone you know—if the shoe fits, wear it, if not, toss it out.

I must also mention that sometimes it might not necessary mean that the man himself is bad—*Roaz* represents a spirit of deception or distraction. This spirit is dangerous because it is preventing women from realizing their destiny in God. For example, let's say you were called to for a specific task (which all of us are), and you are single and longing to be in a relationship. You finally get in a relationship, and now you are not going to church consistently, you are involved in things you've never imagined, and you feel your relationship with God is almost nonexistent. This is what happens when the Roaz spirit has it way. You almost become someone else.

When we marry a man and he's not complete in God's love, we are going to encounter more lumps in the clay than we are willing to smooth out. Many of us have the fantasy of getting married and living happily ever after because we have watched those images in Hollywood for so long. We have literally fooled ourselves into believing that this is how marriage is supposed to be. The first time your husband doesn't compliment you, meet you at the door with roses and chocolate, or pay attention to you during a football game, your mind is probably going to tell you that maybe this isn't your knight and shining armor. That's just not reality. The fact is that there are going to be disagreements, arguments, and difficult days. That's just reality. Sadly, many people put much effort into planning the wedding and very little effort into preparing for the marriage. We find the perfect dress, a cathedral-size church, the perfect season; yet, very few people take classes to learn about the subject of marriage. The average couple just hopes that everything will pan out after the honeymoon.

For instance, the first thing that couples usually encounter in marriage is financial issues. This is inevitable if there was an excess amount of money spent on the wedding and honeymoon. The marriage is already starting on shaky grounds when you start off in debt. This goes back to preparation. Finances should have been one of the first issues that should have been addressed before getting married. Some people don't realize that their partner is a compulsive spender until after they have gotten married. Communication and planning must take place in the early stages of the relationship so that the marriage can have a fair chance of survival.

Roaz #1: Michael—"Mr. Excuses"

Meet Michael. Michael represents the first form of Roaz. He's in a committed relationship with Shelly, but the relationship is not going to go anywhere. They have been dating for two years, and he's always makes excuses about why it's not the right time for them to get married. His latest excuse is that he's waiting for Shelly to get her Bachelor's degree in criminal justice so that they can have a stable income, since he already has his masters in broadcast journalism and is working for WKTV. This seems like a noble act, but the only thing Michael is doing is buying time. Shelly won't allow him to move into her one-bedroom apartment with her because it goes against her religious beliefs and upbringing. Michael has lived a good life, coming from a two-parent home, and he still has the ability to live with his parents in their three-story home. He doesn't see the urgency to get married because he has everything he needs, or so he thinks. His parents are helping him to live well by providing him a luxurious style of living so he can remain GQ and drive his brand-new BMW and dress in his fine linen suits. Although she has reservations about him moving in with her, she is fulfilling his sexual pleasures. He's also helping her pay her rent and car note, so this also makes him a keeper in her perspective. Michael is content with where he is, and he will continue to make excuses as to why he's not ready to be married. He appears to be such a good man when he buys Shelly a chocolate diamond engagement ring for her birthday. The only problem is that they did not set a wedding date. Shelly's life will continue to be on hold because Michael hasn't yet revealed that he is happy with the relationship just as it is. The truth of the matter is that "Mr. Excuses" is really afraid of responsibility.

Roaz #2: Keith—"Mr. Already Committed"

Meet Keith, "Mr. Already Committed." Keith has been married to Stephanie for five years, and he has been dating Kelly for three years. Keith married Stephanie after he found out that she was pregnant with their first child, Christian. Keith loved Stephanie, but he didn't necessarily want her as his wife because she was not on the same level education-wise. Keith was a pediatrician, and Stephanie was still working on an AA degree at the local community college. Keith was attracted to Stephanie because she had long, wavy hair, a nice personality, and a Christian upbringing. Her parents also pastored Tanner Chapel Baptist Church, a small church in their local town. Keith didn't necessarily grow up in the church, but he knew God and prayed when he had to. Keith and Stephanie began to have problems at home because Stephanie was spending excessively and barely cooking dinner. Keith was frustrated because he was the breadwinner, and Stephanie's only responsibility was to take care of the house and Christian during the day and attend her one class at night. Keith started frequenting the local

Barnes and Noble to relax and have a latte and a light snack. During one of his visits one day, he noticed Kelly. Kelly was a nurse for the local hospital, but she was struggling financially because her daughter's dad refused to help her financially because he was involved with someone else who had a child. Kelly was in the children's section, reading *Where the Wild Things Are* to her daughter. She was a regular customer at that particular Barnes and Noble as well. She had noticed Keith and even thought he was handsome, but once she saw his wedding ring, she just took her focus off him. As she and her daughter were leaving the bookstore one day, Keith approached her and asked if she had a pediatrician for her daughter. Kelly was in shock because she had just called the insurance company, requesting to change her daughter's doctor. She informed him that she was looking for another pediatrician because her current pediatrician had too many patients. He handed her a business card, and she didn't realize until she got home that he had also left his personal cell phone number and a little note that said, "Call me when you can."

After following all the procedures for changing her daughter's doctor, she finally scheduled an appointment with Keith. She was amazed with the level of professionalism and care that he provided for her daughter. Before she left the doctor's office, Keith pulled Kelly aside and asked that she give him a call after 5 PM. Two weeks went by, and in one of her desperate moments, Kelly called Keith. They talked for hours about how unhappy he was, and about him needing someone he could relate to better. He made it seem as though Stephanie rode a broomstick by the absurd comments he was making about her, like her being inconsiderate, selfish, and angry all the time. Stephanie just so happened to be out of town for a women's retreat. They finally met up on a Friday and ended up spending the weekend in a hotel together. They were officially a couple after several more dates and sexual encounters.

Keith now had a family on the side. He'd already won Kelly over by promising to divorce his wife. He attended her family events and split holidays between his wife and Kelly. He spent quality time with her daughter, and she actually cried when he left. They had gotten comfortable being together in public. Stephanie was aware of the extramarital affair after about a year, but Keith kept her happy at home by buying her big-ticket items (a car, jewelry, etc.) and providing frequent shopping sprees. Kelly was accustomed to the lifestyle Keith was providing for her as well. She was no longer living in a cramped, one-bedroom apartment because she was now a homeowner in a gated community. Keith spent three nights out of the week at her house, and four nights with his wife.

This form of Roaz is selfish, and his tactic is to make everyone happy in this foolish situation. He will not divorce Stephanie, and he will keep Kelly as long as she wants to be kept. Mr. Already Committed is happy just the way things are. This type of Roaz will show up in a subtle way and catch you off guard if you are not careful. Once you get involved with someone who is already committed through marriage or another relationship, it will be very painful when it does end.

One of the most admired figures in the Bible—David—struggled with the sin of adultery. He blew it by the world's standards, yet he is noted, even today, as a man after God's own heart. If you read Psalms 51, you will discover that not only did David realize that he messed up, but he confessed it. He didn't beat around the bush and say, "If I sinned, I think I have sinned," but he acknowledged his sin immediately and received deliverance. Too often we play patty-cake with sin, and we don't acknowledge sin as sin. We tend to say things like, "I made a boo-boo, or an oopsie, or I slipped." No! No! No! Admit you sinned, bottom line, end of discussion, and now you must repent. Many of us miss the mark when it comes to repenting, or we really don't understand what it means. According to *Vine's Expository Dictionary*, repent means to change one's mind, to change direction, thinking, or course of action. Please take notice of the definition which lets you know that there is some action that needs to take place on your behalf—this isn't just lip service.

Roaz #3: Floyd—"Mr. Down Low"

Meet Floyd, another form of Roaz, aka "Mr. Down Low." Floyd had a difficult childhood, to say the least. He grew up in a home without a father, and his mother was partying too much to ever pay him enough attention to see what was really going on with him. During one of the nights him mom decided to go to the local club, Patches, she decided to take him to one of her friend's houses two blocks away. His mom would leave him with neighborhood sitters periodically so that she could go to various clubs. This particular night, she left him at her friend Patty's house. Patty's eighteen-year-old son, Fred, was still living at home, and he had a reputation for molesting little boys, although it hadn't been proven because all of his victims were too afraid to speak out. That night, Fred came into the room where Floyd was sleeping and violated him.

Too ashamed to tell anyone for years, the shame and guilt haunted Floyd into his adulthood. He struggled with his sexuality in college and had a couple encounters with men, especially when he was going through initiation into his fraternity. He tried to dismiss the feelings that he had for men, but they just wouldn't go away. Floyd was an attractive man with hazel eyes and curly, jet black hair, and he was a suave dresser. He was voted King of the University during his senior year, and he had more females than he could count. He finally ended up becoming serious with Tina, and they end up getting married.

Meanwhile, since he never received counseling or ever dealt with the issue of being molested, he was still feeling the need to be with a man. He was a great husband to Tina in the first two years of their marriage. They would take vacations together with other couples, they would frequent fancy restaurants, and they were living a rather generous lifestyle, being that both of them had received their business degrees and were working for Fortune 500 companies. During their third year of marriage, the sex stopped completely. Floyd no longer desired his wife sexually. He stopped complimenting her, and he basically started avoiding her by working late and scheduling out-of-town trips.

Tina decided that she was not going to allow the enemy to destroy her marriage. She went to church sometimes, but she wasn't what you would call a "churchgoer." She did know that prayer worked. One day, she decided to go to Victoria's Secret and find the sexiest lingerie available. She put on nice jazz music over a candlelit dinner, and Floyd wasps into the house late as ever with an attitude. He didn't even glance over at Tina to see her dressed like a holiday package just for him. When she got into bed to caress him, he just didn't even respond. By now, Tina was bitter, angry, and despondent. She tried to talk, but it only ended up in an argument.

Their home basically turned into an apartment living situation, because they ended up sleeping in separate bedrooms. The marriage was falling apart, but none of their family and friends realized it because on the outside, it appeared as if they were functioning like a normal family. Another year had gone by now, and Tina was at the point that she could not continue to live this way. She recognized that something had to change. She finally scheduled several appointments for counseling, and after several sessions, Floyd finally disclosed to Tina that he was no longer in love.

After going through the motions, Tina began to question herself and work harder on her personal appearance and wifely duties, not recognizing that all of this was just in vain. One day, while Floyd was in the shower, his phone beeped with a text message. The text message stated that the sender could not wait to see him in the next hour. The womanly instinct kicks in, and Tina decides to give the sender of the message a phone call so that she can finally call his mistress on the red carpet. After dialing the number, her heart feels as though it's beating a million beats per minute as she waits to give this woman a piece of her mind. The sender picks up the phone, and Tina discovers that it's not a woman but a man text messaging her husband. Her husband has been involved in an extramarital affair with another man. Tina was married to Floyd, "An Undercover Brother."

This form of Roaz, "Mr. Down Low," realizes that if he doesn't get married, his family is going to eventually put him on the suspect list, so he does the unthinkable—marries a woman when he is not sure of his sexuality. These types of men are usually very successful, but they realize coming out of the closet could desperately damage their career, so they use marriage as a cover-up. Tina had no idea that she was marrying this type of man. Through counseling and really opening up during the dating stage, these issues could have been confronted. This is not only happening with common people, but Hollywood is infested with such marriages, and because people aren't sensitive to the voice of the Holy Spirit, Christian women are not exempt from this type of madness.

Roaz #4: Fabian—"Mr. Potential"

Meet Fabian. Fabian grew up in a single-parent home, but his mom worked hard to make sure he had the best of everything while he was growing up. He attended private school, and he was able to mix and mingle with his middle-class friends without feeling intimidated. He grew up with his father being in and out of his life, so the only real role models he had were his uncles, who owned a local mechanic shop. Fabian was athletic in high school, and he was the quarterback for Leon High School in his local town. By the time he graduated high school, he had received several scholarship offers, but he decided to stay in Tallahassee, Florida, and attend Florida State University. Things were going really well for Fabian at FSU. He had several girlfriends, but by his junior year, he had met Tasha and decided to settle down. Tasha was majoring in engineering, and she too had come from a single-parent home, but she was determined to be successful. By the time Fabian reached his junior year in college, he had injured his knee, and it got to the point that he was no longer able to play football. Not only was his dream of being a star NFL player slowly going down the drain, but his desire to continue in school had diminished. Tasha was soon approaching graduation, and by this time, Fabian had began talking about marriage. He assured Tasha that he would regain his momentum and finish school as soon as they got married. Tasha finally graduated and, believing in her man, she decided to marry Fabian, knowing that he did not have a job.

After a year of marriage had gone by, Fabian still hadn't found employment, and nor had he enrolled back in school. Tasha decided to apply for a loan to help him open a detailing business, since this was something that he had enjoyed doing while in college. After six months, Fabian decided that the job was too strenuous and that he really need to take some time to think about what he really wanted to do. After the fourth year of being married to Fabian, and with him still not finding a job, Tasha realized that she had married Fabian's potential. One mistake that we as woman have to take note of is that what you see is what you get. It is possible for an individual to change, but don't expect a miracle overnight.

After Fabian injured himself in college and realized that he would not be able to go to the NFL, all of his hopes and dreams went down the drain. This form of Roaz is one who seems promising; however, whoever marries this type of guy is basically marrying potential. He is full of great ideas, but nothing ever seems to materialize.

When you encounter this form of Roaz, he is most likely a college graduate, but unfortunately he's the type of person who graduated from college just to make his parents proud and because in his family college is inevitable. He is the type of man who starts everything and finishes nothing. He will be very excited when he tells you about his latest venture, but your follow-up conversation will most likely end in an altercation. His MO is something like this: "Baby, I want to start this business, but there's a $15,000 start-up fee." "Honey, just give me some time, I really haven't quite found my niche yet." "I've researched this project that is going to make us millionaires, you'll see!" This Roaz will give you more excuses than the law allows, and this type of man will end up basically riding on your coattail. You will end up being the breadwinner. He will constantly start promising projects, only to come up empty. If you give in to this type of Roaz, unfortunately, my sister, you just married potential.

Roaz #5: Fred—"Mr. Out of Season"

Meet Fred. Fred is the form of Roaz who is considered out of season. Fred grew up in a family that always had a lot of drama going on. His mother and father were together, but his dad was known as the town drunk, and his mother was a stay-at-home mom who worked hard to care for ten children. Fred did not graduate from college—he was just known as a hardworking man who worked at Faygo's, a local factory that made bottle caps. He earned a decent salary, and he managed to meet educated women and maintain good, solid relationships. He ended up marrying Carmen, a girl with whom he had graduated high school, but she had gone away to Spelman for college.

Carmen was a schoolteacher who came from a prominent family in Atlanta. Her dad was a pastor for Ebenezzar Baptist Church, and her mom was a retired elementary school principal. Carmen was an only child, and she was used to having things her way. When she married Fred, he catered to her every need in an effort to please her. He even worked a second job to maintain her expensive lifestyle. Carmen ended up getting pregnant with twins, and she fell into a major depression. There wasn't anything that Fred could do to satisfy Carmen. Although they were going to Carmen's dad's church every Sunday, their marriage was slowly deteriorating. Fred was becoming stressed, and eventually his doctor placed him on blood pressure pills. Fred decided one day that he wanted a divorce, but he wanted it to be amicable. Carmen agreed to the divorce but requested alimony and child support. Fred, frustrated and anxious at the same time, agreed to the terms of the divorce.

Six months after the divorce, Fred met Monica, who happened to be a teacher. They began spending time together, and their relationship began to blossom. Monica knew that Fred was a good man, but at the same time she realized that if they really became serious, Fred would definitely be considered "out of season." He was still healing from his divorce, and he was drowning in financial debt as a result of the divorce. Although Fred would make a great husband someday, if Monica got involved with him during this season in his life, she was going to encounter several problems, especially on the behalf of his ex-wife.

If you encounter this form of Roaz, he really is a good guy, but you have met him at a time when the season is just not right. He is a godly man who loves and serves the Lord, but he has some issues that need to be addressed before getting married. He may be dealing with financial issues, or he may sometimes exhibit selfish behaviors unknowingly. He may be struggling with letting go of what happened in past relationships. If you are interested in maintaining a healthy relationship with this type of man, you will definitely have to wait. If you do not allow God to complete his work in him, what started out to be a good man could possibly turn into a "Nightmare on Elm Street." This type of man is still on the potter's wheel, and once God finishes with him, he will qualify as a Boaz. He must go through a pruning process before he's ready to take on the role of husband. Marrying this type of man would be like a woman having a premature baby. She's excited that she's finally given birth, but there are going to be some sleepless night, extra medical care will be needed, and the baby will need lots of tender, loving care. This type will produce frustration, and you will not reap the full benefits of a marital relationship.

Roaz #6: Ralph—"Mr. Explosive"

Meet Ralph, aka "Mr. Explosive." Ralph grew up with both parents in the home, but his family was very dysfunctional. They went to church every Sunday and, as a matter of fact, his dad was the chairman of the deacon board at First Baptist Rock of Ages Church. He lined the hymns every Sunday and was admired by many, especially the women. He was a sharp dresser, and he had a smile that would just melt your heart away. It was no secret that Ralph's dad was dating the choir director on the side. As a matter of fact, she would buy Ralph a toy every Christmas.

Evelyn, Ralph's mom, was very passive, and she worked hard to please her husband. She wasn't the most attractive woman, but she loved her family. She was brought up with the school of thought that a woman was to respect her husband no matter what, and leaving him was never an option. Ralph's dad was abusive, and he would often come home after work and start arguments with Ralph's mom. The argument would always end up with Ralph's mom having a black eye or a bloody nose. Ralph, seeing his parents' marriage as his example, carried the same school of thought into his marriage with Patricia.

What started off as a marriage made in heaven turned into a nightmare. Patricia and Ralph married after both of them had gone away to college and then returned to their hometown and church. They reconnected at a single's fellowship, and a year later they were married. They had gone to counseling with the pastor, but Ralph never disclosed how seeing his dad beat his mom had affected him. Patricia had seen him get angry and drive off, but he had never hit her before. The first incident when Ralph became really angry and hit Patricia was when she came in late one night after going to Red Lobster with her girlfriends. He was waiting by the door when she returned. Instead of asking her why she was late, he slapped her immediately. More shocked than anything, Patricia just took her shower, crying as the water hit her then-numb body.

When she got out the shower, Ralph greeted her with a kiss, and he made love to her. Patricia, confused and upset, woke up the next morning and tried to discuss the events that had happened on the previous day. The only explanation he could give her was that when he got angry, he lost control. The anger outbursts and abuse continued, and Patricia tried to seek help for Ralph to help him deal with his past and his anger issues, but he was determined that he would be able to work through it on his own. After four years of being married to Ralph and being abused, one day Patricia finally disclosed to her family what had been going on during her marriage. Her brothers packed her belongings and moved her into one of the family's homes. Patricia divorced Ralph and began going to counseling to help her deal with the abuse she experienced in the marriage.

If you meet this type of Roaz, it will appear that he has everything together. You two may seem like a match made in heaven in the eyes of others. When people see you together in public, they will view you as the couple on the church fan. He will be a regular attendee of church and may also serve in a form of leadership in the church. Most of the men in church look up to him and admire his professionalism, charisma, and dedication to the Lord. Some women in the church may even look at you with envy, wishing their husband was just like yours. The only problem is that when you go home and close the door, "Mr. Explosive" has some anger issues, and he sometimes uses you as a punching bag. This is a sensitive issue that needs to be addressed, and, yes, it is going on today, even in our churches. He appeared to have it all together. You saw some signs in the beginning, but you just ignored them, hoping they would disappear at some point. You probably thought that if you just loved and supported him, everything would work out fine. If you are in one of these types of relationships, put the book down immediately and seek help. You can contact your nearest domestic violence shelter, or if you are in immediate danger, please call the police, and they will provide you with a safe haven. This is a serious situation that needs immediate attention. Silence is not golden when your very life could possibly be in danger.

Roaz #7: Byron—"Mr. Psycho Bob"

Meet Byron, the last form of Roaz. His surname is "Psycho Bob." Byron came from a family where his mom was known as the town drunk, and she was known for having sex with men to support her drinking habit. His father was still married to his mother, but he lived in Texas, hundreds of miles away from Byron and his nine sisters and brothers. His mom became an alcoholic after his dad left her for another woman. The family experienced extreme poverty once Byron's dad left the family. Byron would find himself stealing cookies and potato chips from the local convenience store to help relieve his hunger pangs. By the time Byron turned thirteen, he had already left home, dropped out of school, and was having sex with older women. He would sleep with older women so that he would have somewhere to sleep at night. After all, he was slender and handsome, he had chestnut-colored eyes, and he had lots of charm, so he could win his way in to a woman's heart, even at the tender age of thirteen. By the time he was sixteen years old, he worked side jobs until he earned enough money to catch a train to Chicago. Although he had dropped out of school, he was ambitious and intelligent, and he still longed for a better life. He slept on the streets of Chicago for a while, and he finally found a job that let him pay room and board to a gay man he had met while working at a store as a bag boy. During the weeks he could not pay rent, he would have sex with the man in exchange for the amount he owed for rent.

Byron finally received a job at a fast food restaurant, and because of his customer service skills and his ability to multitask, he was moved up to a management position in a year. He performed his job duties so well that he moved up to district manager in three years. This was when his problems began—he started going to parties with the colleagues, and he was offered pure cocaine. After getting high for the first time, he began desiring the cocaine daily, but the only problem was that he could not afford the real cocaine. He ended up getting addicted to crack cocaine and losing everything, including his job.

He spent most of his adult life fighting the drug addiction, but he was able to work for himself and earn as much as $80,000 a year. His childhood still haunted him, and everything within him was trying to work hard to make sure that he had a better life. He ended up in a condominium, driving a convertible mustang, and wearing fine clothes. Once he stabilized himself, he met Tiffany. Tiffany was younger than Byron, and she had also come from a single-parent home, where she had experienced sexual abuse, poverty, and some of the things Byron had experienced, so they connected immediately. Tiffany hadn't been exposed to drugs, so she really didn't know the signs of a person using drugs. After all, she was fresh out of college and still learning about the real life.

They dated for six months before getting married, and once they got married, Tiffany's world was turned upside down. Byron became a different person. He began staying out late or not coming home at all. He would start arguments with Tiffany so that he could get angry and go get high. One day he came home demanding the money out of their bank account because he owed the money to drug dealers. Tiffany would come home and find the televisions and other electronic equipment gone. One day while she was sleeping, he took her car and pawned it off to the drug dealers. Tiffany was too ashamed to tell her family and friends what was going on. Tiffany was faithful at church and heavily involved with the choir and mission group. Byron would come to church every now and then, when he hadn't been out on a binge.

If you looked at the couple, you would think they were living a good life because they were neatly groomed, lived in a nice home, and both of them had fine cars. The truth of the matter was that their home life was nothing short of a living hell. Byron had isolated Tiffany from her family and friends, and he was controlling her every move. Tiffany finally convinced Byron to get counseling as a couple to try to save the marriage. The counselor informed Tiffany that his unresolved issues in his past were his biggest enemy. Tiffany attended Narcotics Anonymous with Byron with the hope of supporting him and helping him to kick his habit, but he would go back out and use. After being married two years, Tiffany discovered that she was pregnant with their first child. The stress and the instability almost caused her to lose the baby. She had to be placed on bed rest for the majority of the pregnancy. After their son was born, she thought that being a father would be enough to kick his habit, but things got worse. Tiffany was growing weary in the marriage by the time the baby had turned two years old, and she was trying to find a way to escape from the marriage. Byron had already told her that if she ever tried to leave him, he would kill her.

By this time, it was do or die for Tiffany—she wanted out. She and the baby were sleeping in the guest bedroom, and she was disconnecting herself from Byron. He came in and had sex with her one night against her wishes, and to her surprise she found out that she was pregnant again. She was upset, despondent, and depressed because she felt like she was stuck. After the second baby was born and she went through the same complications as the first pregnancy, Tiffany was at her wit's end. She was so miserable that she felt herself losing the desire to even live.

When the baby was nine months old, she did the most courageous thing ever—she left Byron. She drove four hours away to her mom's house. After being there for two months, she filed for divorce, and the divorce was granted six months later. Tiffany joined her home church, became active in ministry, and God begin to heal her heart and open up doors for her. She ended up receiving a teaching position that allowed her to get her own apartment and start over again.

This form of Roaz makes a decent salary, but you are going to need the majority of the money for counseling when he's done with you. He will start off sending you flowers and showering you with very expensive gifts early on in the relationship, but this is not without a cost. As soon as you decide that you don't want to march to his beat, he will most likely demand the gifts back. He is constantly using money as a means to control others. He doesn't feel powerful unless he has a plenty of money in the bank. This Roaz does not love God or himself, so he is definitely not going to know how to love you. He most likely has a poor relationship with his own mother or father or both. He probably overlooked the Scripture that says, "Honor your father and mother," which is the first commandment with a promise: "that it may go well with you and that you may enjoy long life on the earth" (Ephesians 6:2, 3). There are so many people today walking around not blessed because they have forgotten that this commandment contains a promise to live long or die prematurely.

When you first meet Psycho Bob, he is going to approach you from a religious standpoint. He will probably tell you that he is actually called into the ministry, especially if you seem to be a super-spiritual sister. That is a lie from the pit of hell. Most likely, this type of Roaz hasn't even answered the call of salvation. Psycho Bob is bound and has several issues, and once he gets you, he will most likely let you know that no one else will ever have you. He will say this in a joking manner, but he will mean it literally. If you marry this type of Roaz, if he's not physically abusive, he will definitely say hurtful things and will try to make you feel unworthy, such as saying things like, "No one else is going to want you, anyway."

Psycho Bob will be anxious to get married. You will probably marry him at the courthouse because he wants it to be quick and easy. If you have good credit, he will most likely put everything in your name. The debts you owe will supersede your annual salary. Psycho Bob's next scheme will be to isolate you from friends and loved ones. He will most likely cut off any meaningful friendships or relationships that you may have. Every time you introduce him to one of your close friends, he will begin criticizing and assassinating the person's character. He tries to dismantle any meaningful relationship so that all your attention will be strictly on him. Psycho Bob also loves it when your family does not live in the same city, and he really celebrates when they live in different states. This strategy is important to him, because he wants to make sure that he has you all to himself so that he can control you in every way he can.

The most dangerous thing that this type of Roaz will do is attempt to distract your relationship with Christ. Once you get married, he will most likely complain about you going to church and Bible study. If you are involved in any type of ministry at all, he will call you a hypocrite and claim that you are spending too much time at church.

It will be difficult to break free from this type Roaz because he will become very angry if he finds out you are trying to leave him. You most likely will have to seek outside help to dissolve this type of relationship because your life can literally be in danger, especially if he makes statements like, "If I can't have you, no one else will." This type of Roaz can end up causing you to lose your life if you are not careful. If you have encountered a person who exhibits these types of traits, please pray this prayer with me:

Prayer:
Father God in the name of Jesus. I have entered an unhealthy relationship against your will. Father the Holy Spirit warned me about this relationship when I first met _____, but I continued to ignore the signs. Father, you came to give liberty, yet I feel so bound in this relationship. I literally feel as though I am loosing myself in this relationship. Father, I am asking in the name of Jesus that you make a way for me to escape right now in the name of Jesus. Father, your word declares that you will never leave me and never forsake me. Your word also declares that you have not given me the spirit of fear, but of power, love, and a sound mind. Lord, it is not your desire for me to live in fear, so I am releasing my faith that you will deliver me from this ungodly relationship in the name of Jesus. I take the first step by making a decision to leave this relationship. I trust that you have something better in store for me. Today I make the decision to wait on you. Father, these and other blessings I pray in Jesus name, Amen. (If this doesn't apply to you, intercede for someone you know.)

Chapter 4:
How Did I End Up Here with Roaz?

Does God still have a plan for my life
although I have messed some things up?

For I know the thoughts that I think towards you, saith the Lord, thoughts of peace, and not of evil, to give you an expected end (Jeremiah 29:11)

There are so many women wondering how they ended up in relationships that were short-term, abusive, or just plain unfruitful. They question their ability to make sound decisions because they figure, "I am educated, I'm a Christian, and I am a good-looking woman—how could it be that I can't attract a godly man?" They see sister Katrina, who's just an average-looking woman, but she has a handsome, educated, Christian man who treats her like a queen. These types of couples are seen all the time in the mall, at church, at the movies. Deep down inside, it makes you angry because you know that you are more than qualified to get a good catch.

You have been active in church, attending all of the single's events and conferences, and yet, you are still coming up empty. You still end up with the man who wants to have sex, take you out to dinner on his terms, and answer your calls or text when he feels like it. Basically, you are attracting Roaz, who is not looking for commitment but for a good time. Let's look at four possible reasons why these types of men keep showing up in your life.

1. Impure Motives

   Many women will fast and pray for a husband, but their reason for wanting a husband is not the right reason. For example, some women are not looking for a husband—they are really looking for a "sugar daddy," a man who will pay all of their bills, buy them expensive gifts, and give them access to the bank account. A woman wrote an ad in the personal section of the newspaper that said something to the effect of, "If you can't take care of me, don't respond." Having this type of motive or attitude will never yield a godly husband. You will attract a "Roaz" who will string you along, and you will think that you are getting over. In the end, you will need counseling because you have chosen a lifestyle that will cost you later since you have put yourself in a position that will cost you emotionally. There is no need to look for a sugar daddy when God is ready to supply all your needs according to his riches and glory through Christ Jesus. He is Jehovah Jireh!

2. Anxiety

   Then you have women on the other end of the
   spectrum—they are so anxious to be married
   that they will do whatever it takes just to have a
   man. You have women doing ridiculous things like
   proposing to the man, moving their things into his
   house without his permission, paying his bills, or
   demanding him to marry her or else. In some cities,
   such as Atlanta, there are more women than men,
   and women have found themselves in compromising
   positions because they are anxious to have a man
   or be married. It doesn't matter what the statistics
   say—what God has for you, it is for you. The
   Bible admonishes us, "Be anxious for nothing, but
   by everything by prayer and thanksgiving, make
   your requests known unto him. (Phillipians 4:6).

3. Lack of Self-Love

   There are women who are suffering today from
   lack of self-love. The amazing thing about
   it is that they are beautiful, hardworking,
   professional women who have not recognized
   that they do not love themselves. Well, how can
   such a strong statement like that be made? It's
   evident in the way they allow men to treat them.
   They end up in relationships with men who are
   already committed, they think their outward
   beauty or good sex is going to keep the man, or
   they settle for a man who constantly takes in the
   relationship and gives nothing in return.

If you ask the average woman if she loves herself, she would probably look at you crazy for even asking that question. Her response would probably be, "Can't you tell I love myself? I drive the best, live in the best, and eat the best." This may all be true, but it's not evidence of self-love at all. Many people judge self-love on the way they treat themselves; they rarely dig deeper and notice how they allow others to treat them. This is equally important. Lack of self-love will definitely yield a Roaz-type man. Believe what God says about you: "You are fearfully and wonderfully made" (Psalms 139:14).

4. Lack of Knowledge

If you were to survey the average person to find out if they had a proper example of a healthy, happy marriage, you would probably hear more no's than yeses. Marriages used to last thirty and forty years because the couples were in it for the long haul. The sacredness and preciousness of marriage has been lost along the way, leaving many lost on how to go about obtaining a mate the proper way. There are so many people who are allowing Hollywood to give them information about being married, and some are using talk shows such as *Oprah Winfrey* and *Dr. Phil*. I'm pretty sure that there are some areas on which these talk shows may be able to give some helpful hints; however, the Bible is the most resourceful. If you purchase an item and expect it to function properly, then you usually take it back to the manufacturer if it does not. The same thing is true of marriage. If you need answers regarding marriage, then the proper thing to do would be to go back to the creator of marriage—God. God created marriage, so he just might know how it is supposed to function. That's just like me buying a computer from Toshiba and calling the cable company when it malfunctions. That doesn't make sense at all, but, unfortunately, that's what's happening. The Bible states, "My people are destroyed for lack of knowledge" (Hosea 4:6), and, most importantly, "In all thy getting, get understanding (Proverbs 4:7). Women are ending up in relationships with Roaz because they lack the necessary knowledge of what it takes to receive a godly man. They have to learn to be like Ruth—although you are waiting, you are waiting with a purpose. You are educating yourself on marriage and positioning yourself to receive Boaz.

Chapter 5:
Faith's Story:
Ugly Duckling Syndrome

People think that you are confident and maybe even beautiful, but deep within, you have a poor self-image and subconsciously you feel as though you will never find anyone to love you for you.

Why do I continue to date these guys only to find out that they are cheating on me?

And be not conformed to this world, but be ye transformed by the renewing of your mind, that ye may prove what is that good, and acceptable, and perfect, will of God (Romans 12:2).

"I cannot believe that this man is cheating on me," Faith said as she looked at the black mascara that had smeared like charcoal on her dark chocolate skin. Her eyes were nearly closed from the puffiness that adorned her face. Her bobbed-cut, straggly hair didn't help her self-image as she looked in the mirror, desperately wondering where she had gone wrong. I mean, why wouldn't a man want her? After all, she was dark with smooth skin, had perfect white teeth, was fine and fit, and although she had four children, she was still educated and on top of her game. She had a Doctorate degree in educational leadership, and she exposed her kids to finer things in life, so in her mind she was a good catch.

When she would walk in the club during her partying days, all eyes would be on her because she would have spent three hours in the mall so she could be dressed to impress. All the Ques, Kappas, and Alphas knew her because she had worked on campus while in college, and she was known for her boldness and sassiness. Her thinking was, *Once I put it on a guy and give him sex like he's never had it before, he's not going anywhere because he will be hooked.* The only results that she yielded from that were good-looking men who were bound to cheat. On the outside was this bodacious, sexy, well-put-together, educated woman, but on the inside was this little girl who was battling low self-esteem, a poor self-image, and a distorted image of love. Although she grew up with her mom and dad in the home, her family still struggled financially, and they lived in the type of neighborhood where there would be a drive-by on the regular.

She'd never really seen her daddy show affection toward her mother. They slept in separate beds, and he would go to work, come home, take a shower, and then go to bed. The projects were close by, and you really had to be strapped or "street" in order to survive in the hood.

Faith's first sexual encounter was when she was sixteen, and it was with this big-time drug dealer named "Chico." Faith battled low self-esteem because of her dark skin, and back in the day she would have been called a "Celie" from

The Color Purple. When she was in high school, if you were not of fair skin or have a pecan tan, most of the boys didn't really pay you any attention. Chico did make her feel special, because every time after they had sex he would take her to the mall and buy her an outfit or two. She wanted very badly to be considered pretty for once. After all, her pecan-tan friend Samantha got all the compliments, even from Chico, when they were together, and Faith was just considered the ugly duckling who happened to be hanging with Samantha. Taking the belief of feeling ugly deep down inside, she really wanted to be considered pretty.

Faith tried to cover it up her poor self-image with clothes, an attitude, and success. Her poor self-image and distorted image of love added to her lack of success in relationships. She was taught in the hood that if you do things the average girl wouldn't do, then you will be straight as far as a man is concerned. By the time she had graduated from high school and started college, things were going well, and she thought she had met the man of her dreams, Bobby. Bobby was from Savannah, Georgia. He was a family-oriented, handsome guy who came from a family of educators, and he had high hopes of making Faith his wife one day after discovering that she was pregnant. His upbringing taught him that he was to take care of his responsibility, and he was willing to do that, but Faith's hard-as-nails attitude and ghetto ways had Bobby second-guessing.

After Kayden was born, Faith and Bobby's relationship turned tumultuous. By this time, she was cursing out his family and doing whatever she could to keep Kayden away from him. Bobby loved his son, but he knew that the future with Faith was very dim. He finally ended the relationship with Faith and put himself on child support because he could no longer deal with her outbursts of anger. By the time Faith graduated from college, Bobby was already dating someone else, but Faith would cause scenes whenever she saw them out together at the club, movies, or any public place, for that matter. She would usually call his girlfriend names and make idle threats of bodily harm.

This behavior continued for about a year, until Faith met Steve. Steve was well put together and articulate, not to mention handsome and suave, just like Faith liked them. He would command the attention of the ladies wherever he went, and he did. His brown, smooth skin, curly hair, and 6'5"-225 lbs. attracted women to him immediately. Faith thought she had hit the jackpot with this one. The relationship progressed until she started getting calls from the previous baby mama. Keep in mind, first of all, that he had never mentioned kids, and baby mama drama would definitely set Faith off! Finally, Faith found out she was pregnant with his son. Instead of embracing and comforting her, he began to go out with other women and slip by every now and then for a little sex on the side.

He was no longer answering his phone, and he was going back and forth with the first baby mama. Faith was distraught! She started going back to the club and even decided to get herself a man or two on the side after the baby was born. During one of her moments after the club, she invited Steve over and they had sex. Faith later discovered that she was pregnant with their second child, and now Faith was the single mother of three children. After that, Faith began taking care of him and her three children. She made sure that he had money pay his car note and to keep himself going. One day, she received a call from another lady claiming that she too had a baby with Steve. Faith forgave him and tried to continue to build a relationship with Steve although she had moved to the position of the woman on the side.

A year went by, and all of a sudden Steve moved out of state, and Faith had no idea of his whereabouts. Since her relationship with his family was shaky, she couldn't establish a rapport with them to allow the children to develop a relationship with his family. Sinking deep in debt, depressed, busted, and disgusted, Faith received a job offer to move to Italy rent free, with a fringe benefit package she could not refuse. She packed her belongings and kids and moved to Italy.

Once she moved there, she met a gentleman from Jamaica, and she was intrigued by the way he treated her like a queen. He took her on nice quiet walks in the park, made her breakfast in bed, they went to romantic dinners, and he spent time with the kids—just a pure delight. Six months later, she discovered that he had a family back in the States, and he was only trying to kill time while he was away from his family.

Again, Faith was crushed! Another Roaz! She began to cry out to God. She realized that her relationship had deteriorated with God since she left high school. She remembered how she used to sing in the church choir and pray before she went to bed every night. She realized that after broken relationships, three children, and a feeling of disparity, she had left her first love—Jesus. She called her close friend Clarissa, who she used refer to as super-spiritual-sister, and asked her to pray for her. After talking to a coworker, she and the children were invited to attend her church. Faith became active in the church—she joined the choir, and her children were active in the youth ministry. Faith realized that she had some areas that definitely needed healing, and that she would not enter into a relationship until those areas of self-love and self-esteem had been addressed. Faith participated in the singles activities at her church regularly, but she was not actively seeking a relationship. She was learning the basics of how to prepare to receive the right type of man while waiting with a purpose.

Reflections:

What are some issues that prevented Faith from finding the right mate?

_____

_____

_____

_____

How did Faith's past affect her adulthood as it relates to relationships?

_____

_____

_____

_____

Can you or someone you know relate to Faith, and if so, how?

_____

_____

_____

_____

Pray this prayer for yourself or for someone who reminds you of Faith and her situation.

Prayer:

Dear Heavenly Father, I thank you for helping me to realize that I am in need of your help as it relates to relationships. Forgive me for not acknowledging you in the decisions that I have made in this area. Help me to view myself as you view me, realizing that I am the apple of your eye and I am fearfully and wonderfully made. Help me to accept your good and perfect will for my life in the area of relationships. Prepare me to receive a godly mate that we may bring glory and honor to your name. I break all soul ties with everyone that I've been in a relationship with that was unfruitful. In Jesus name I pray. Amen.

Chapter 6:
Hope's Story:
Woman at the Well Syndrome

Will I ever find someone to love me for me?

Perfect love casteth out fear (I John 4:18).

"My life was never supposed to turn out like this," Hope said as she clenched her fist in anger. She struggled with anger and believed she lacked the ability to forgive. She was angry with herself, angry with life, and, although she didn't want to admit it, angry with God. As a result, she hadn't been to church in a while. She found herself in a backslidden state. All of her friends' lives seem to be going swell, but why did life have to be so hard for her? She was finding men, but the only thing good in the relationship was the sex. The men were never interested in a long-term relationship. She was already struggling with low self-esteem because of her past and her longing to be loved. She was taught that her body was what attracted the right man. This alone disqualified

Hope because she wasn't considered to be what men would call a "brick house."

She was what a man would consider average. She was about 5'3", 140 lbs., and pecan tan with short hair and full lips. She was feisty and demanding, and she had a wall up due to the sexual abuse she had experienced at the tender age of seven. The molestation by her babysitter made her confused, and at times she had questioned her sexuality because of the abuse she had endured. The molestation in her childhood did not make her a lesbian, but it surely made her promiscuous. She never had a problem getting a boyfriend, but she never felt the man loved her for who she really was. In the back of her mind, she knew it was the sex that was keeping them around. The wall she had up would have to be torn down in order for her to receive the love that she so richly desired. She, like the woman at the well, had such a thirst that only God could fulfill it. She found herself quenching that thirst with men.

Hope had encountered different forms of Roaz in her lifetime. She met her first Roaz at the age of fifteen. She was in a college preparation program when she met him. She had already had a sexual encounter by the time she was twelve years old, and that happened because of a dare made between herself and her best friend at the time. Hope had been a promiscuous teen because she really didn't love herself, and her father wasn't there to fulfill some of the voids she had at the time. Xavier, her first Roaz, was unique in that he came from a two-parent home, both his parents were educated, and it appeared that he had a good life. Meanwhile, Hope was living on the opposite side of town with her single mother and sister in a subsidized apartment complex, barely making ends meet.

Hope's mom was in and out of relationships with men that were doing more taking than giving. Hope had already made up in her mind that she would definitely not choose a man who was a taker. She was wooed by this young man, and he literally became her world. He was already sixteen and driving, and he would pick Hope up in his shiny, metallic red Chevy Blazer and take her over to his world. His mother would always have a hot Southern meal prepared, and Hope would always join his family for their sit-down dinners. It was customary in their home that everyone sat down as a family and ate dinner and discussed their day. This was new to Hope, because there were times when she literally didn't have a dinette set to have dinner, so dinner was always on the go in her house. Xavier would pick her up from school, give her money for basic necessities, and also take her on special rendezvous so that they could have sexual encounters.

A year had finally gone by, and Hope was sixteen and Xavier was seventeen. She had entered her junior year in high school, and things appeared to be going along lovely. One day, Hope woke up, and she wasn't feeling so well. She felt nauseated, and it appeared that everything she ate kept coming back up. She felt strange because she wasn't the sickly type, and she usually noticed any changes in her body immediately. In spite of how she felt, she continued to press her way. One day, it finally hit her when she noticed that she was pregnant.

"I'm pregnant," she said to herself softly, and the pregnancy test from Dollar Tree confirmed it. When she got home from school that day, she called Xavier and scheduled a time for them to talk. He came over that afternoon, and Hope never forgot the expression on his face when she quickly mumbled these two words: "I'm pregnant."

The first thing he uttered to her was: "How do you know it's mine?"

Clenching her teeth, she looked at him in anger and said, "Of course it's yours, stupid, I haven't been with anyone else!" She was so hurt by the way he responded to their dilemma. Her knight in shining armor had turned into a different character. She told him that she wanted to keep the baby, and that she wasn't going to have an abortion. He begged and pleaded for her to have an abortion because he was more concerned about the blemish it would put on his family name. After he threatened to commit suicide, she finally gave in, took the $300 he offered, and had an abortion.

She was totally devastated. Eventually, she had to get her mom involved because by this time she was terrified. This would become one of the worst experiences that she would ever encounter. After the abortion, the relationship was back in full swing. Believe it or not, she and Xavier had an on-again-off-again relationship until they reached college. By the time she was nineteen years old, she would have had two more abortions. Although Hope was not religious and did not grow up in the church, she did remember reading in the Bible that thou shalt not kill. She did not want to be branded as a murderer. With Xavier threatening to commit suicide each time she ended up pregnant, Hope was already wearing the label. She would have nightmares about the abortions, and she walked around with guilt and condemnation, not being able to tell her friends and family what was really going on with her.

By the time she started her first year in college, she was already frustrated and not focused, so she decided to join the Air Force. Prior to going to the Air Force, she had a wonderful celebration hosted by her sister prior to being shipped overseas, and who shall appear? You guessed it, Mr. Xavier. They ended up having some serious good-bye sex, and the next day she was off to Korea. She didn't realize that a couple of months later, her very world would be turned upside down.

When she arrived overseas for her first tour of duty, she met Derrick on her new job assignment. She and Derrick began going out to dinner, spending the night together, and enjoying one another's company. In fact, they had become inseparable. One morning, she woke up feeling horrible—she had been down this road before, and she knew that she was pregnant. She scheduled an appointment with the doctor, and after close examination, they confirmed that she was pregnant. Her heart dropped just like the previous times when she had gotten the pregnancy news. She shared the news with her Derrick, but she also explained that the baby was most likely for Xavier back home. She finally had the duty of calling Mr. X, and she had already braced herself for the suicide message.

He was now in a new relationship with someone in college, and he had basically gone on with his life, as she had. She explained to him about the pregnancy, and how she believed that the baby was conceived during the goodbye sex encounter. She waited as the suicide message began to flow from his lips: "My parents are not going to be happy with me having a baby out of wedlock; I might as well go ahead and take my own life." By this time she had had it. She explained to him how in no uncertain terms was she terminating the pregnancy. She also volunteered to mail him the rope if he needed to hang himself, because she was having the baby.

By the time she reached her second trimester, she decided to exit the Air Force and move back home. Derrick decided that he wanted to be with her despite of the pregnancy and that they could maintain a long-distance relationship. That worked well for about a month after she left, until one day they had a conversation that would change the fate of their relationship. He decided that he was not comfortable with her having the baby and asked if she could have an abortion. Hope knew that day that the relationship was over. She terminated the relationship with Derrick, and she didn't hear from him again. She gave birth to a healthy baby boy that summer, and she didn't regret having her beautiful son. Xavier went through the motions of not claiming their son in the beginning. As a matter of fact, his family showed up at the hospital, but Xavier was a no-show. He decided to have a blood test to prolong the time because he was deeply in love with his new girlfriend, Trina.

The blood test came back confirming what Hope already knew, and Xavier began to support his child. Xavier actually left Trina and actually tried to become a family by the time their son turned two years old. He had moved some of his things into her one-bedroom apartment, and he took care of most of the bills. By this time, Hope began going to church and establishing a relationship with God, and she explained to Xavier that it was time to settle down and get married. Xavier, still really not wanting to make any real commitments, started going through the motions. The first thing he did was buy Hope a promise ring to appease her and so that they could continue having sex since they were headed toward marriage. At the time, Hope was in college working on a BS degree in criminology, and Xavier had already obtained his degree in broadcast journalism.

The next reason Xavier gave for delay in marriage was because he told Hope she really needed to finish college so that they could have two stable incomes. Hope was so motivated by the new challenge that she finished a four-year degree in three years. Now that's motivation enough. A few months after Hope graduated from college, she found Xavier cheating on her with the same girl whose phone number was found in his pocket on Valentine's Day. To appease Hope and assure her that he was committed to their family, Xavier decided that he would leave his parents' home and move in fully with Hope and their son. Xavier continued to play the field. She would continuously find receipts from restaurants, phone numbers—you name it, and she found it. Xavier was interested in saving his family, yet his desire for other women was constantly pulling him in other directions. Losing the battle to his flesh, his last appeal was to claim he would buy them a home. Hope didn't wait around for his broken promises.

By this time, she had already made up in her mind that she was out of there. After graduating from college, Hope accepted the first position in her field out of state. Needless to say, Xavier ended up marrying one of the women with whom he was cheating with. He then had the nerve to say that she shouldn't have left, and that she should have given him time to sow his royal oats—huh! It was finally etched in Hope's mind that a selfish man would not commit if all his desires were met during the dating stage of the relationship.

Reflections:
What are some issues that prevented Hope from finding true love?

_____

_____

_____

_____

How did Hope's past affect her adulthood as it relates to relationships?

_____

_____

_____

_____

Can you or someone you know relate to Hope, and if so how?

_____

_____

_____

_____

Please pray this prayer for you or anyone you know who is having sex with someone who says that it's okay because you all are going to get married anyway.

Prayer:
Father God in the name of Jesus. I pray for _____, who is involved in a relationship of deception. Lord, I pray that you will forgive _____ for having sex outside of the covenant of marriage. Father God, I pray that you prepare _____ to receive her Boaz. Father, help her to be able to recognize him when he comes because their relationship will be based on spiritual things instead of things of the flesh. The man you send for _____ will love you, Lord, more than he loves _____ and himself. He will willingly wait for their wedding night to seal their union. Lord, I pray that _____ will release any soul ties from previous relationships so that none of them will enter into her new relationship. Father, I thank you for your delivering power and your forgiveness, and most of all, I thank you that whom the son sets free is free indeed. I declare _____ free in Jesus name, Amen!

Chapter 7:
Charity's Story:
The Materialism Spirit

What's wrong with wanting the finer things in life even if you have to go through some things to get them?

For what does it profit a man to gain the whole world and lose his soul (Matthew 16:26)?

"I can't believe that I'm walking away with my children and the clothes on my back," Charity thought to herself as she loaded her truck and kids and headed to live with her mom. Not healing from a previous relationship properly, Charity ended up with the worst possible Roaz. It all started when Charity moved to a new city. She had just graduated from college and was starting her career.

It was a breezy day in October when her sister and her best friend came into town to visit for a couple of days. They had just left a carnival, and Charity's sister and best friend decided that they wanted fancy acrylic nails like the ones she was wearing. She drove them to the nail/barbershop, which happened to be down the street from where they were. The shop was owned by a friend Charity had met during the short time she had lived there.

As they waited for Darla, the nail tech, to finish her sister's nails, Charity began gazing out of the shop's window. All of a sudden, she saw this nicely groomed guy pull up in a black convertible mustang, looking cool as ever. They guy appeared to be a little bit older than she, and he looked to be a sharp dresser. By this time, her best friend had joined her in watching the sporty guy park his convertible.

They both began to laugh because in his attempt to look cool and suave, he ended up hitting a yellow stump in the parking space. Nonchalantly, he proceeded to enter the shop and demanded to be next in the barber's chair. Apparently he was a great tipper, because all of the barbers were talking about him before he entered the shop, and he could pretty much demand what he wanted from the barber. As he was getting a haircut, Charity began to feel someone staring at her. She looked up, and it was Mr. Special who had demanded to have his hair cut right away. When he finished getting his haircut, he bid everyone farewell and proceeded to walk to his car.

Charity's sister had finished getting her nails done, so they ended up leaving soon after Mr. Special. Charity walked outside, and she saw the guy motioning for her best friend to come over. Charity made jokes as her best friend proceeded to walk toward him. By this time, she thought that he was trying to flirt with her best friend. Her best friend came back over with a number in her hand, and she proceeded to hand it to Charity. She looked astonished because she had no idea that he was interested in her—after all, she wasn't looking for a man at all.

That evening, on a whim, she finally called him, and they ended up staying on the phone until three o'clock in the morning. He basically gave her his whole life story, and she found herself able to relate to him in a lot of ways when it came to childhood issues. He finally asked her out for a date. She agreed to go on date with the stipulation that her sister and her best friend would have to accompany them. He picked them up and took them to a nearby comedy club. All seemed well; he was happy, and her sister and her best friend were satisfied (they were ordering alcoholic beverages like crazy on his tab). Finally, the night concluded, and he took them back home. Charity decided to hang around and talk to him some more outside in the car.

They talked for a while, and she thanked him for everything. He asked Charity for a second date. This time he wanted the date to be them alone. Charity paused for a moment because although they had talked over the phone, she still wasn't comfortable being alone with him by herself. But she agreed.

She planned the perfect date—Disney World in Orlando, Florida, being that it was only two hours away. Charity had read that when you were beginning to date someone, theme parks were great because you were not in a situation where people aren't around if something went down. After this date, he appeared to start getting really serious, and he began to come on really strong. He started leaving angry messages when she wouldn't pick up the phone, and she started showing up at her apartment unannounced. He even sent flowers to her job, requesting to see her. By this time, she was becoming a little bit hesitant, and she wanted to break it off because he was getting a little bit too serious.

She called him and explained to him how she felt the relationship was moving at a faster pace than she would like it to be moving. She explained to him that she did not want to see him anymore. *He hit the roof!* He began calling her job and calling the phone at home, leaving wild and crazy messages. One day, he left one message too many, because he actually made a threat on this particular message. By this time, Charity realized that she had really met a Psycho Bob. She was literally horrified. She decided to get the police involved because the message was actually life threatening. After the police listened to the message, they arrested him the next day for aggravated stalking. Apparently, the police knew who he was and had had an encounter with him because of his cocky attitude.

He went to jail for a few days, and when he got out, he had the audacity to call Charity and beg her to drop the charges. Charity felt really bad, and of course she decided to drop the charges. However, the only problem was that the state had picked up the charges. He apologized to her and promised that he would give her some space. He tried to plead his case of how he really wasn't a bad person, how he had just really grown to like her, and how he didn't like the fact that she ended the relationship abruptly, especially after he had shelled out so much money over the time since they had met.

Charity forgave him and even began to date him, thinking that if she provided him with some sort of stability, she could change him. Charity knew deep within that this was not the right thing to do, but she totally ignored the Holy Spirit.

She attended church regularly, and she knew when God was speaking to her. Charity knew that she hadn't healed from her previous relationship, and that she shouldn't be entertaining another relationship at all. After dating him for six months, he asked her to marry him. Charity agreed; after all, she was growing tired of struggling to pay her bills and raising her daughter alone. He started attending church with her, and he really embraced her daughter, who was from a previous relationship. He would buy many expensive gifts for her daughter, take her to school frequently, and spend quality time with her regularly. He had definitely won her daughter over. Charity's mother and father were hesitant when they first met him, but due to the fact that he had won her daughter over, they just went along with the program grudgingly.

When it was time for them to start their marriage counseling classes, he was excited. Unfortunately, after the counseling session, the pastor pulled her aside and explained to her that he didn't feel as though she was ready for marriage. The pastor decided not to marry the couple because he felt that they were on two different levels spiritually. Not agreeing with the pastor, Keith decided that they should join another church. After being at the church a couple of months, Charity befriended her Sunday school teacher, who was also a circuit court judge. She asked her friend to marry them in her chamber. Charity could tell that her friend really didn't want to, but she wanted her to be happy.

They were married in her friend's chamber, and after that, all hell broke loose. Part of her husband's past included drug use, and it began to resurface. Charity thought that the issue of drug use had already been resolved and that was just a part of his past. He relapsed within one month of the couple getting married. Charity literally found herself going to crack houses looking for him before she went to work. She was devastated because she had never been around any hardcore drugs except for marijuana, and she had no idea about crack or addicts. All of her vacation time for her job was spent dealing with issues related to her husband's addiction.

As if it couldn't get any worse, Charity found out that she was pregnant with this addict's baby. She was excited at first because her daughter was not born from a marriage, and she thought that her husband would be just as excited about the pregnancy. He responded in such a way that really crushed Charity. He already had three other kids, and he looked at having another child as a burden. Charity had several complications during the pregnancy, mainly stemming from stress. On the day she went into labor, her husband Keith was out smoking crack. It was by the grace of God that he sobered up enough to take her to the hospital. She was so embarrassed when she got to the hospital.

There she was, a respectable person in the community, and she was having a baby from a man who reeked of alcohol and drugs. In spite of his addiction, God's grace allowed him to buy everything the baby possibly needed prior to coming home. He was an excellent provider, but, boy, was there a price to be paid.

Nine months after their son was born, Charity was frustrated with her husband. At that point, she had gotten so many restraining orders and gone to court so many times, she was exhausted. Charity literally felt as though she was losing herself. One day, she was in the tub crying out to God.

She was in so much pain at the time that she begged God to literally take her life.

As soon as the thought of dying left her, she came back to her right mind. All of a sudden, she got a burst of supernatural strength and decided that she would live and not die. When she decided that she was going to live, she packed her belongings, called her best friend, loaded a U-Haul, and moved back home. She divorced Keith. Meanwhile, everything was going swell at home, and she began working on her law degree. One of the men from a previous relationship began trying to come back into her life although he was married. After going to church and hearing a wonderful sermon on the woman's role in the marriage, Charity evaluated her first marriage and convinced herself that she didn't do all that she could have done as a wife. She began talking to her ex-husband, Keith, and he convinced her that he had been clean for over a year and was stable and ready to come back and get his family. Charity wasn't really happy with her job at the time, and she was yearning for change, so she allowed her ex-husband to pack up their belongings and move to the city where he was living. Everything was going swell—he was paying the bills, and she was looking for a job.

One day, things begin to take a turn. She heard him talking to another woman one night on the phone, and he actually left the house to go sleep with the woman. Apparently, he had been involved with the woman prior to Charity moving there. She was hurt, speechless, and angry. She packed her belongings again, got her children, secured a job, and decided that she was out of there. After collecting a couple months' wages, she moved to an apartment near her job.

A couple of months later, Keith lost the beautiful apartment in the affluent neighborhood where they had been living and literally became homeless. His addiction escalated, and his life was going down the drain. He called Charity one night and asked if he could please come and stay the night because he didn't have money to pay for a hotel. She agreed to let him stay as long as he agreed to stay out of her bedroom.

On about the second night, she found him in her bed, and he tried to have intercourse with her while she was sleeping. He literally penetrated her, and when she awoke he had basically reached his climax. From this act, she later discovered that she was pregnant with baby number two from him, so now she was preparing to become the mother of three children. Of course, not wanting the pressure of having to raise three children by herself, she tried to work on a relationship with Keith, hoping that he would change. Charity began desiring to have a home since the family was increasing. She finally began searching for homes. The homes she found within her price range were basically fixer-uppers, and she did not have the patience for turning a matchbox into a mansion. Keith found a decent home, provided the money for the down payment, and all was going well. Charity and Keith married a second time three days after the purchase of the home.

The marriage was even worse the second time. He was at the heart of his addiction. It became hard for him to stay clean from day to day. By this time, everything that wasn't paid for with cash was in Charity's name. They had accumulated a lot of debt, and Keith would only work just enough to get by. If he wasn't smoking his crack, he was on the computer for hours at a time, playing spades. Charity was so miserable that she didn't know what to do. It was finally time to have the baby. He was there during the birth, and this time he had just came off a drug binge when he got the news that she was about to deliver. He sobered up and came to the hospital prior to delivery. She had an emergency C-section and was in a lot of pain when she got home. Keith stayed near the home front for the first week, but after that, he was back to his drugs and the internet. By that time, Charity had lost her ability to feel emotionally. She didn't desire or want to nurture the newborn baby.

She was scared out of her mind because she was fearful that the drug dealers were going to come and kill the whole family. She had begun to live a life of fear. It was so bad by this time that she was trying to find a way to go crazy. She had reached the point where she wanted to take Keith out or end her own life. Depression had crept in to the point that she didn't have the energy or desire to take a bath or care for her children. Charity had reached a point of no return and, again, she had had enough. She and the children checked in at a local hotel, and she decided to take the greatest risk ever. She made up in her my mind that she was willing to lose it all. She would gladly give it all up because she was miserable. She called the police and had them meet me her at the house because by this time she had a restraining order on Keith, and he refused to leave the house.

She gathered some important papers, herself, and the children, and as the children proceeded to get some of their toys, Keith made them put them back. Her children were devastated. She stayed in a hotel three days prior to making the four-hour drive back home. She tied up some loose ends, including abruptly leaving her job and turning off and closing accounts related to the house. When she arrived home, her three children took the few items that belonged to them and crammed it all in her mother's one-bedroom apartment. She spent the first couple of days just numb. She didn't interact with anyone, not even the kids. She felt like a big block of ice needing to thaw out. By week three, she began getting herself together, and the Holy Spirit revealed to her that the only way that she could receive healing was to reach outside of herself and help someone else. Her mission began!

She began to go to an area where homeless people were present, and she began to take them lunch daily and talk to them as if she herself wasn't officially homeless. She felt herself getting stronger day by day. She became heavily involved in her children's school, and she volunteered frequently, serving as a parent leader. By the second month, a job literally dropped in her lap. She was called in for an interview and hired on the spot. Things were beginning to look up. By the third month, she moved into her own apartment. God allowed her to fully furnish the apartment, and their wardrobe was finally beginning to grow. She began to receiving financial blessings from friends and family, and she found a Word of Faith ministry, where she began to grow.

She tried to attend the traditional Baptist church that she was accustomed to, but she realize that she needed more than just the feel-good Sunday morning experience. She needed something that would slay some of the giants that she was facing during the week. She was broken and in need of serious healing, so she found a church that would destroy every yoke of bondage. The ministry she joined literally gave her new life.

Charity realized that only God could change man, and that you cannot override man's will. Although she may have had good intentions in wanting to be married, she also discovered that if you don't allow God to heal you in his timing, you can end up with an undesirable outcome that can cost you everything in the long run. Wait up on the Lord—again, I say, wait.

Reflections:
What are some issues that prevented Charity from finding true love?

_____

_____

_____

_____

_____

How did Charity's past affect her adulthood as it relates to relationships?

_____

_____

_____

_____

_____

Can you or someone you know relate to Charity, and if so, how?

_____

_____

_____

_____

_____

Please pray this prayer for yourself or for someone you know who may be in a similar situation.

Prayer:

Father God, I thank you that you are a God who is forgiving. I realize that you hate divorce, but you love me. Cleanse and purge me right now, so that I may exhibit forgiveness toward my ex-husband. Take away the painful memories of the past. Help me to realize the part I played in causing the marriage to fail, and help me to repent. Help me to walk in love no matter what. Cover my children, and let the peace of God rest and rule in their heart. Allow your healing and delivering power to be manifested in my life, so that I may be a blessing to others. Thank you, Lord, for giving me several chances. In Jesus name I pray. Amen.

Chapter 8:
Desires & the Non-Negotiables

Will God honor my requests?

Be careful for nothing; but in everything by prayer and supplication with thanksgiving let your requests be made known unto God (Philippians 4:6).

Many women have faltered in relationships because they know that they want to have a happy, healthy relationship; however, they have not set standards as far as what they want in a relationship. There are some who may think that you are egotistical, bourgeois, or really overreacting; conversely, how are you going to recognize what you want, if you have not written down a vision for what you want? When people are planning on building a home from the ground up, they contact an architect, they tell him/her what they want, and the architect designs a blueprint based on what the potential homeowner desires. These are spiritual principles as well. Habakkuk 2:2 states, "And the Lord answered me, and said,

"Write the vision, and make it plain upon tables, that he may run that readeth it."

Now, for all the Bible scholars, Habakkuk was a prophet when the Babylonians were in power. Habakkuk was making a complaint regarding injustice, and the Lord replied to Habakkuk in Habakkuk 2. The Bible was written for our learning, and we can take the same principles and apply them to our everyday lives. Everything that I've obtained in life has been through a matter of writing things down and using Scripture to stand on. The nonnegotiables list is important because it requires some soul searching. It requires looking deep within to discover things that you are not willing to tolerate. I know that we are dealing with imperfect people because we are flawed, but it's important to know what you want, know what you don't want, write it down, and pray over it. Only you know what you are willing to tolerate. Had I done this prior to getting married, he and I probably wouldn't have even gone out for ice cream. Below, I have given an example of my desires & nonnegotiables list. The desires list is just what it says—desires. The nonnegotiable list is a simply a guide. You have to determine what you consider a deal breaker.

Reflections:

Now you pray and search within and create your own person list of desires/nonnegotiables. This will prevent years of heartache and pain. This simple activity will keep you focused, and once you meet Boaz, he will be easily recognizable because you have made this simple list. If you are already married, you may still complete the activity and pray for your current spouse, and you can turn yours into a prayer journal.

My Desires	Nonnegotiables
Spiritually Grounded	Smoker
Honest	Excessive Drinker
Neatly Groomed	Abusive
Financially Stable	Married/Committed
Family Oriented	Liar
Educated	Drug Abuser
Self-Confident	Unstable
Humorous	Non-Tither
Musically Inclined	Manipulative
Visionary	Unmotivated

Chapter 9:
How to Attract Boaz

What must I do in order to attract a man such as Boaz?

"Trust in the Lord with all thing heart; and lean not unto thine own understanding" (Proverbs 3:5).

There are some very key principles which we must understand in order to prepare ourselves to attract Boaz.

Principle #1
Principle #1—we must be born again. If you have not asked Christ to come into your heart, then that must be first and foremost. You cannot bypass God and his institution and expect success. First of all, God is love. To leave God out of the equation is doing the same thing people who are unbelievers do for Christmas. It's like having a birthday party without inviting the honoree. Sounds absurd, doesn't it? But that's what people do when they are unbelievers and they get married. This may shock you, but God is not your father if

you are an unbeliever—Satan is your father. So since God is love, and love is God, you can read John 3:16 like this: "So Love so loved the world that he gave his only begotten son, so that whoever believes in Love, may have everlasting Love." Everywhere in the Bible that you see the word "God," replace it with the word "Love."

So, by principle #1, you must be born again. Romans 10:9 declares " that if you confess with your mouth and believe in your heart, that God hath raised him from the dead, thou shalt you shall be saved." It didn't say if you feel something, roll on the floor three times and jump up and down. It's a simple profession that seals the deal and changes your destination from hell to heaven.

Principle #2

Principle #2—we must know who we are in Christ. We will never experience true victory until the "In Christ Message" becomes a revelation. Many of us have a distorted image of who we really are in Christ. We haven't exactly allowed the "In Christ Message" to sink in totally. As a matter of fact, until you understand who you are in Christ, you really do not have the right to request Boaz. You cannot expect God to send heaven's best when you don't even know who you are. If you meditate on some of the following Scriptures and say them consistently, it will help you develop your image of who you really are in Christ: I Cor 1:30, 2 Cor 5:19, Gal 3:26, Eph 1:3, Phil 3:13, 14, I Thes 5:18, and Phlm 1:6.

So, by principle #2, know who you are in Christ. The Bible provides an example of how God truly sees us. Through reading the Scriptures continually and praying for understanding, you will be able to allow the word of God to become real in your life. Once the word becomes real in you, the manifestations of who you truly are will shine forth.

Principle #3
Principle # 3—we must allow the man to be attracted to the God in us. Anything you attract in the flesh will have to be maintained through the flesh. If you go back to the Book of Ruth and evaluate what she did while waiting for Boaz, we can really learn a lot from her. One thing she wasn't was desperate. She wasn't going around the field dressed like a hoochie mama trying to attract Boaz—she maintained her grace and femininity. She didn't glean in the field with dazzy dukes and spaghetti straps—she really adorned herself in the garments of holiness. Many women spend so much time on their outer appearance that they forget to build up their inner woman. Building the inner woman involves reading God's word daily, praying continually, and developing a relationship with God. For example, the woman in the club is not the type a woman that a godly man is usually attracted to. The godly man is attracted to the woman who has power. For example, if he experiences death in his family, he's not going to be thinking about how sexy his wife is—he's going to be more interested in a woman who can pray him through difficult situations. This is why the outward appearance cannot be the major priority. It's the God in you that will sustain the relationship.

Principle #4
Principle #4—please forgive all those men from your past who have hurt you. Unforgiveness is like you drinking

poison with the expectation that someone else will die. Unforgiveness is like cancer—it will continue to eat away at you until there's nothing else left. You must forget those things that are behind you and press toward the mark of a higher calling in Christ Jesus (Philippians 3:13). Many women are finding themselves alone because they cannot let go of things that have happened to them in the past. There is another group of women who are making their current mate pay for what men in their previous relationships did to them. How can God truly forgive you and wipe your slate clean when you are holding unforgiveness in your heart? As much as God loves you, he cannot violate his principles to pacify you. So, by principle #4, you must forgive. The chances of attracting Boaz are slim to none if you are carrying any unforgiveness in your heart.

Principle #5
Principle # 5—submit to God. Submitting to God requires that you find out what God requires of you, and then you must choose to obey. If you are having difficulty submitting to God as a single person, it is impossible to submit to your husband. Many marriages are falling apart today because they think that submission is a dirty word. The husband is using the word as a power tool to control the wife, and the wife is having flashbacks from the slavery days. Both people are misinformed because the true meaning of submission is "to fall under." The husband is the head over the wife, meaning that he gets his orders from God and conveys the message to his wife. It doesn't mean the wife is lower than the husband, because they are both equal in the sight of God. God is a

God of order. During the time of singlehood, submitting to God will include spending time in his word, developing a relationship, and obeying God's word immediately. A part of that submission includes consulting God in every situation pertaining to your life. A woman submitted to her God truly will be a crown of glory for her husband. So, by principle # 5, submit to God.

Principle #6
Principle #6—get your house in order. This not only pertains to cleaning, washing dishes, and cooking. Yes, these are important, but get your affairs in order. Learn balance before you allow this new relationship in your life. If you are already struggling with your day-to-day duties, inviting someone into your life might end up being stressful instead of a blessing. Just as a woman who is pregnant has to make room for the new addition that will be entering the home, the same principle exists for the single woman who is expecting to get married. Think about all the things that takes place before the baby is born, and apply the same principles in receiving a husband. So, by principle # 6, get your house in order.

Principle #7
Principle #7—spend time in God's presence by praying. Everything you receive on this earth will be birthed by way of prayer. Begin by praying for yourself and declaring Scriptures over your husband. Prayer will be the very glue that holds your marriage together. Develop a devotional time when it's just you and God, and transfer that same habit to your marriage. You will find that you will have sweat-less victories

by developing a meaningful prayer life. So, by principle #7, spend time praying in God's presence.

Principle #8

Principle #8—get involved in workshops and conferences at your local church, and get connected with individuals who are already successful in marriages. You are in the preparation stage, and of course the Bible is your number-one source. You could definitely benefit from reading and attending some workshops or conferences pertaining to marriage. The more you know, the more you grow. You definitely don't want to base your marriage on how Hollywood handles marriages. Talk shows are great; however, they don't provide enough sustenance to maintain your marriage.

Most churches have marriage ministries as well. It is a good idea to attend some of the meetings and ask questions of people who are actually successful in the area of marriage. It's not a good idea to get advice from individuals who have a negative view of marriage or have given up on their marriage. If it's your desire to get married, God will put the right people in your life to guide you as well. So, by principle #8, get involved in workshops and conferences, and connect with successful married couples.

Principle #9

Principle # 9—maintain self-discipline. We know that we live in this world, but we are not of this world. The world says, "Have sex before marriage so you won't be disappointed when you get married." When we have sex before marriage, we take away the opportunity for both the man and the woman to develop. It takes away the ability to develop because having sex before marriage increases the appetite for sex. Once you start having sex, it becomes increasingly difficult to stop.

Another area that has become prevalent is cohabitating prior to marriage. Usually when couples choose this type living situation, it seems as if the relationship would excel; however, the exact opposite happens. Because there is no commitment through marriage, either party can decide at any time that they want to leave. Self-discipline says that you honor what the Bible says, and you choose to follow, even when it's difficult. So, by principal #9, maintain self-discipline.

Principle #10
Principal #10—we must understand agape love. Many of us have been taught to love based on conditions. Agape love says, "I love you not based on conditions or circumstances." It also says that there is nothing that you can do to make me stop loving you. This type of love is rare, and it can't be mustered up on our own. It takes the power of the Holy Ghost to manifest this type of love because it's not natural. This is the type of love that will sustain any type of relationship. When you are able to exercise the agape love that's given once you become born again, you will be able to position yourself to attract Boaz. So, by principle #10, you must understand agape love, the God kind of love.

Chapter 10:
Marriage 101:
The Maintenance Program

Are there any blessings obtained through marriage?

Whoso findeth a wife findeth a good thing, and obtaineth favour of the Lord (Proverbs 18:22).

Now that you've received some guidance on the way to finding your Boaz, it's important that when and if you obtain Boaz, you are able to maintain a positive, healthy relationship. There are several blessings that are associated with being married—it's as if a fringe benefit package came along with the marriage. Some of the fringe benefits include working together to fight the enemy, teaming up to fulfill the call of God in each of your lives, having a sexually fulfilling relationship that's not based on selfishness, raising children in a two-parent home, and growing old with someone with whom you are able to make wonderful memories. These are just a few of the many blessings that you will experience.

In an effort to keep your marriage strong and healthy, you must develop some sort of marriage maintenance program. For example, in the case of a vehicle, if you don't follow the maintenance program, your car will not last as long as it was originally designed to last. The same principle is applicable to marriage.

Everyone's marriage maintenance program may not be necessary identical. However, you as a couple must determine what's going to work well in your marriage. After interviewing five couples (friends, family members, and therapists) who considered themselves to have happy, successful marriages, here are some common items that were found in their plan:

1. A date night once a week.
2. A time to pray and study the Bible together regularly.
3. A time to enjoy individual activities, and agreement to quickly forgive one another when offended.
4. A weekly family night if kids are involved.
5. Regular attendance of church and Bible study.
6. A pact to fight fair, which means no demeaning remarks during arguments.
7. Keeping family and friends out of their business.
8. Contact the other partner when spending over a certain amount of money.
9. Addressing the problem when it first arises.
10. Agree not to argue in bed—this is the place of intimacy.

One thing that married couples must also realize is that they will experience greater attacks once they are married. After the honeymoon period is over, couples must put on the whole armor of God, as outlined in Ephesians 6, so that they can withstand all the wiles of the devil. It is important that the devil not be allowed to get a foothold in any area of the marriage. One area that's vitally important that some women tend to do once they have obtained Boaz is to stop looking their best. Don't get me wrong—when Boaz found Ruth, she was busy working, but she had to have had it going on. If you don't believe me, check this out—she had to prepare herself before she went into Boaz's presence. "Wash thyself therefore, and anoint thee, and put thy raiment upon thee, and get thee down to the floor" (Ruth 3:3). Ruth, being a submitted woman of God, listened to her mother-in-law and dressed herself up when she went to see Boaz. We are spiritual beings, but we still live in a body whose senses are fully operable, so we just can't let ourselves go now that we've obtained the prize.

Honor is the key to the blessing. Women must honor their Boaz as priest of the home and not disrespect him. Married couples sometimes forget that their partner is not only their husband or wife, but they are their brother or sister in Christ. If this truth is kept in the forefront of our minds, we won't be so quick to dishonor one another.

Build your husband up as often as you can. "Life and death are in the power of the tongue" (Proverbs 18:21). Speak life into him every opportunity you get. It will be especially important when he comes home from work. Whether he works in business for himself or is employed for a company, the home should be his fortress. He should feel like the king of the castle when he arrives home. If you have children, set the tone before he arrives. Make sure that they are not screaming and destroying the house before your husband arrives. No one wants to come home to an environment that looks like a hurricane has hit it once or twice. Give him time to unwind when he comes home before sharing all of your concerns of the day. Women, we have the power to make man reach his greatest potential. I'm almost certain that if there was no Michelle Obama, there would be no Barack Obama—excuse the incorrect grammar, but you get the point.

There is a saying: "What happens if Vegas, stays in Vegas." Keep what goes on in your household, in your household. Do not engage family members or friends in your household affairs and problems. This will cause destruction in a marriage faster than a tornado. If you decide not to take the high road, your husband will be the center of ridicule at the next family gathering. You would have made up with your husband, loving on him, and just in marital bliss, while other people are judging your husband based on the negative image you've painted of him.

Marriage is one of the most beautiful institutions that God has created on the earth. Marriage was meant to be heaven on earth. Marriage is getting a bad rap in today's society because it's getting to the point that it's no longer honorable to be married. It has gotten to the point that people change partners as often as they change cars. There are instances where people have to get a divorce because their lives are in danger, but many people are leaving marriages to pursue other people because they have "fallen out of love" with their spouse or they just prefer to be single. These are some of the reasons that have been prevalent through watching family and friends' failed marriages.

There is hope in the area of marriage. The single woman need not be discouraged in the area of finding a mate. It does require hard work, dedication, and two committed individuals, but it can be happy and healthy. The symbol of love in a marriage is a wedding ring. The wedding ring can either be a symbol of undying love for your spouse or a shackle. It can be a shackle because if you choose the wrong mate, it can be a weight. Think about how you may have things going on in your life before you get married, and now imagine adding more weights to your already existing problems. This will indeed make life difficult. After salvation, marriage is one of the biggest decisions that we will make in life. Since it is a lifelong commitment, and since we have to wait a little longer than we really want to, we can wait with a purpose. We can serve God, achieve our goals, and maintain a pure heart while waiting for our Boaz.

Poems to Ponder

By Anastasia Means-Dallas
(Allow each of these poems to minister to you in a special way.)

***

The Counterfeit

Thinking I was the real one you chose too soon
I was never the one I knew I had you fooled
I possessed all the characteristics in the
beginning that a woman would love
All along I had you thinking I was sent from above
You thought I was there to do you
good for the rest of your days
You even postponed your dreams,
and accepted many delays
Waiting for me, hoping someday that I would change
You should have recognized that I was a
fake when I started to run game
I knew that I had you in the palm of my hand,
But because of your brokenness you would not take a stand
I'm sorry to disappoint you, because I'm
really not fit to be your man
Even I knew that you deserved better,
and that's the reason why I ran.

***

Lonely

How can one feel lonely when people are all around?
It's hard to imagine that it can hit you even in a crowd
A spirit indeed that causes self-pity
And if you toil with it too long, it
will sort of make you dizzy
Causing your head to spin because you
long to have someone around
But because you weren't specific when you
prayed, the results were profound
That spirit of loneliness crying from within
Hoping to find a relationship that can soon begin
Attracting someone that should have never had a chance
The person you allowed in your life
wasn't even worthy of a dance
To allow him to partake of privileges not yet earned
Is setting yourself up for failure that could
have possibly been discerned
But because you gave in to the flesh
and did not wait on God
Now the spirit of loneliness has attracted
someone who is putting up a façade
Saying that he loves you, because he
found you in a desperate state
And now that the light has come, you
realize that he's not your soul mate.

***

Spirit of Materialism

Seeking the finer things in life seems to
be some single women's theme
The only problem that lies with that, is
that your source is not the King
Jesus died for us so that we could enjoy an abundant life
But unfortunately we have looked to a man
to provide when we're not his wife
At times we have been guilty of seeking
the Father's hand and not his face
As a result we have missed out on obtaining things by grace
When we look to man to fill our cup
and lust for things in this world
We find ourselves living below the
standards of being daddy's little girl
The truth of the matter is that depending on
a man is like chasing after the wind
You will find yourself with nothing left,
yet you will be sinking deep in sin
Jehovah Jireh is there to provide everything you need
Put your trust in him and not in a man,
and then you will succeed
The riches he offers come with love
and you will never thirst again
Leave your pot at the well and follow him,
and you will have a story to tell.
Trying to recover from the wounds of a painful
past can sometimes weigh you down

Wounds still fresh and heart still broken
can cause your flesh to drown
The act of forgiveness is somewhat buried
in the midst of all your tears
It's sometimes hard to let go when you feel you
have been a victim for over twenty years
Starting new relationships have added
onto the pain that you first felt
Because you have unresolved issues and deep inside
you don't like the hand you've been dealt
Allowing men in your life who are really as broken as you
If you put the both of you together,
it still will not equal two
The healing you seek, as a matter of
fact, can only be found above
Confess to him and watch him cleanse,
and be perfected in his love.

***

Shortage

Who claims there is a shortage when he
owns cattle on a thousand hills?
But many women have believed that he's a god of
not enough when it comes to finding a man
If God did it once, he'll do it twice; so
what if your best friend just wed
There's still a godly man left for you if you
would only prepare yourself instead
This is the same god who promised to
give you the desires of your heart
Why are you so anxious when he told you to
pray and believe right from the start?
Shortage, I don't think so, my god is too big for that
Who put him in a box and doubted him
lots when he said I will fulfill
Live your life to the fullest and enjoy it,
it doesn't matter where you stay
So what you live in Atlanta, Georgia, where
many of the men are said to be gay
I've told you once, I've told you twice—my god will make a way
Even if your prayer is for a godly man
to have on your arm someday
Wait on God and be of good cheer, he's
already overcome the world
I wish women would realize that God is sincere
when he thinks of you as his girl.

***

Waiting

Waiting on God is not a difficult task when
you are waiting with a purpose
You won't be moved when situations and
things actually begin to surface
Many grow weary during this period
because they are mainly staying still
They didn't realize that after the prayer
it's not time you need to kill
Waiting is an attitude after you have
already released your faith
This lesson is also pertinent when you are seeking a mate
Many put off dreams and goals during
this period of waiting
Not realizing that during this season
it's not good for hesitation
Buying the dream home, car, or
business can still be your vision
Don't wait around until Boaz comes, when
God has already made provision
Truly they that wait upon the Lord
shall renew their strength
This is true of every time you're waiting for any length
Remained focused, use time wisely
because God is never ever late
Stop gazing at your watch or looking at your
clock because God's timing is truly amazing!

***

It's Not Negotiable

Settling is not an option for those who
know their purpose in life
It is not in the vocabulary of a godly woman
who is seeking to become a wife
There are standards that must be in place
that a man must surely uphold
It's when we realize that we are valuable
that we can stand and be that bold
No, it's not negotiable if you don't have a
job, a car, or you just can't provide
It is definitely not cool if you are depending
on someone else to give you a ride
No, it's not negotiable if you still have a wife, and
certainly not negotiable if you live a life of strife
Staying out all night and saying you
are hanging with friends
Just to find another phone number
in your pocket once again
It's not negotiable if you can't be a man of
integrity and always bear the truth
You will find yourself being a counterfeit Boaz
when I'm exhibiting the character of Ruth
Too many times we let our guard down
and accept things as they are
Not realizing that compromising our
standards will only leave a scar
To thyself be true is a motto that we all can quote so well

But why do we compromise our standards and
date someone who's heading straight to hell
No, you can't change a man, what you see is what you get
If the Holy Spirit can't get his attention,
what makes you think you're Ms. It?
No, it's not negotiable if your God is not Jehovah
No false gods will I ever serve
That's how I know this relationship is over.

***

Now That You Found Me

Now that you found me, I will do you
good for the rest of your days
Committing not only to you, but to God,
allowing him to direct my ways
Catching you in the spirit as I lift you up
in prayer each morning that I arise
Kissing you and holding you and making
each day a brand new surprise
Not taking you for granted, I promise
you, darling, that I will not do
Words cannot express, actions can only
show this love I have for you
My heart skips a beat every time I
see that smile on your face
Every day I am waiting, anticipating,
welcoming your warm embrace
Pampering you is my pleasure, and treating
you like a king is all I ever dream
I continue to show my respect an honor
just like before I accepted your ring
Our maintenance program of what it
takes to make our marriage grow
I'm so honored to have you as a friend and
mate; thank God it's not for show
When I said "I do," I didn't skip the
line of "till death do us part"
I love you now, always, and forever;
you're embedded in my heart.

About the Author

Anastasia Means-Dallas is a resident of Atlanta, Georgia. She grew up in Tallahassee, Florida, with her mom (Deborah Bowman), and her sister (Ericka Jackson). Reared in a single-parent home, it was the help of her mother's family, the Bowman family, and her grandmother, Alice Stringfellow, that molded and shaped her into the woman she is today.

She has been an educator for over thirteen years, and she is currently an educator in the Dekalb County school system. She received her Elementary Education Degree from Florida A&M University, a Masters in Reading from Nova Southeastern University, and she's currently a doctoral student at Nova Southeastern University.